# Palette

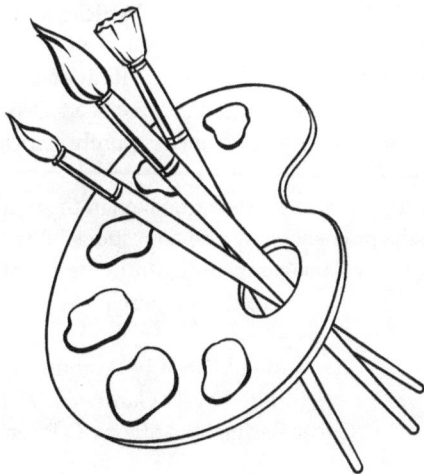

*Love Poems and Painted Words*
## ANTONIA WANG

Other books by Antonia Wang:

Love Bites: Poetry & Prose (2019)
In the Posh Cocoon: Poetry and Bits of Life (2020)
Hindsight 2020: Brief Reflections on a Long Year (2021)
*Retrospectiva 2020: Reflexiones breves sobre un año largo (2021)*
Things I Could Have Said in One Line But Didn't (2023)
*Matices: Poemas de amor y paisajes del alma (2023)*

*Palette: Love Poems and Painted Words*
*Copyright © 2022 Antonia Wang*

*Palette* is a work of fiction. Any names, locations, organizations, and
products are works of fiction or have been used in a fictitious
context. Any resemblance is purely coincidental.

While every precaution has been taken in the preparation of this
book, the publisher assumes no responsibility for errors or
omissions, or for damages resulting from the use of the information
contained herein.

Written and published by Antonia Wang
Edited by Ty Gardner
Cover Design by Anthony O'Brien

First paperback, hardcover and ebook editions: April 2022

ISBN: 979-8-9860457-0-2 (ebook)
ISBN: 979-8-9860457-1-9 (paperback)
ISBN: 979-8-9860457-2-6 (hardcover)

Library of Congress Control Number: 2022906096

Manufactured in the United States of America
biteslove.com

"Beauty is my raison d'être. I live to recognize, nurture, and share it. If it escapes me, I can turn my gaze or retrain my heart. It may camouflage with the grays of the day, but colors seem more nuanced once I find it."

~ Antonia Wang

# Contents:

Part I: Portraits................................. Page 9

Part II: Landscapes .......................... Page 95

Part III: Still Lifes ............................ Page 167


Acknowledgments .......................... Page 219

Illustration Credits .......................... Page 220

About the Author ........................... Page 221

# Part I: Portraits

I don't wear my heart on my sleeve. That would mean it escaped my chest and showed itself to everyone. I hold my heart in my hands: red, raw, and intentional, its frailty eclipsed from the sun by lunar mist, and my arms extended fully in your direction.

# Burns like Flames

He smells like mimosa and indulgence
with hints of delirium.

He is slick like aloe on bronzed skin,
opaque as syrup.

He is fresh like mint against my tongue,
and light as helium.

He speaks like whimsy, burns like flames,
and feels like freedom.


He moves like decadence on glut,
sly as a chameleon.

His hands are arnica and tonic,
stroking tedium.

His eyes are decoys for deep shadows.
I will misread him.

He is keen as hunger and devours me
little by little.

Part I: Portraits

# Stinging Nettle Dreams

She with aurora on her cheeks,
dons yesterday's blush
and tomorrow's green.

She with the wind-tied tongue
and stinging nettle dreams
gently plucked with leather gloves,
and left to wilt under moonbeam…

She of the wholesome mornings,
the unsparing spoon,
and the bites you miss…

# Exploding Dandelions

Every time I think of you,
dandelions spread
in my sunken chest.
I weed them all but the one
where you kept your heart
from the prying wind—
doubt trapped in your eyes
with the finality
of the twilight sun,
love unraveled
into lucid ether…
like a puff.[1]

---

[1] Originally published in FromOneLine Anthology, Vol. I

Part I: Portraits

# Through Your Eyes

I taste your ennui,
while the city rains in sepia
through your wistful window.

Downpours of yesterday
wrest me from a thought,
and the intoxicating petrichor
lures me to your tired piano
as it mumbles and moans
an ordinary note.

It sounds *sui generis*
swelling from your hands.
Those blue-veined streaks
couldn't mar their charm.

For a moment, I see the world
through your vintage eyes.

And although I can't touch the ghosts
concealed by umbrellas
on your bistro streets,
I cry for my own,
for the wretched wraiths
I cannot see.

# Unmistakable

I do not know an eagle
from a falcon in mid-flight,
nor can I see the translucent borders
parceling our skies.

I am not sure why my eyes water
on most cloudy days,

but when my heart rings
at the fork of another road
and my chest bursts open,
I know you are home.

# They're All Yours

You sought I love yous
as if they were home
for hummingbirds
on their way to summer,

and I gave them to you
because I had more
popping sores
under my wings.

I gave them all to you
because they were heavy,
and breeding and drunk,
dragging down my silken wings.

# The Art of Joy

The art of joy between my toes
after I mourned you a thousand sunsets...
Rain on my lashes for every blink
of the muted sky.

Your screams within my hollow,
a raspy echo
lapping at my wrinkled feet—
stuck in the sand.

The craft of unraveling loss
when its crochet stitched my instinct
in cunning patterns where I lie,
snug and warm.

Your scent imbues the yarn
with hues of sorrow
and those blues keep drenching me
at sea and land.

# Seconds like Needles

I strip rainbows,
open empty chests,
bust my brittle wings
out of crumbling nests.

I pluck seconds like needles
from my bare feet
and seek you in meridians
where my spine grows weak.

I walk the orchid field
blooming by your tomb,
praying your spark
will ignite this gloom.

# Mirthless Rouge

In her dreams, he dangles
a set of keys before her eyes.
She does not know behind which door
she left her heart.

Her cheeks are mirthless under the rouge.
She is a flower reft of pride.
Her dress is silk on mended onyx
where weary ravens go to die.

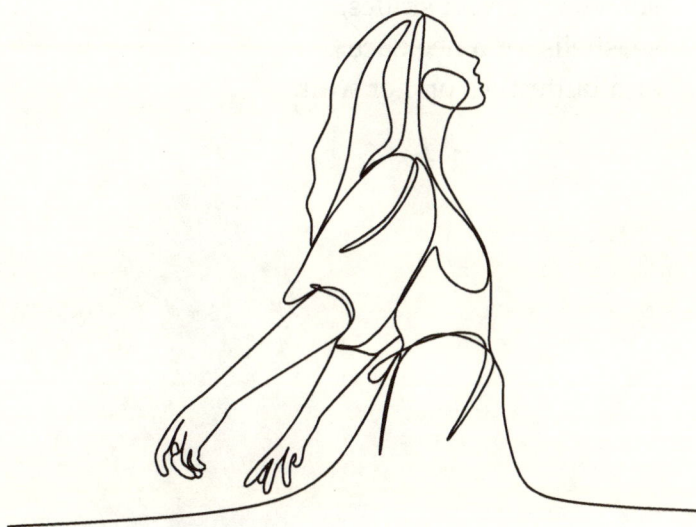

# Daily Ritual

At half-past dawn,
she sips the morning
and reads her teacup
for news of the day.

She dips her lips in coral,
winks to summer,
and sews mustard daisies
on a white sundress.

At half-past dusk,
she wears sweet smiles,
seashells for a necklace,
and butterflies on her wait.

# Glow like Nebulae

I wish to scribe
the cliffs of a rapid pulse
and convey its remorse
to a dying heart.

If I saw the stalls
that feed your lonely mornings,
and the geranium meadows
in which you ride,

I would caress your stride,
and glow like nebulae
in your cosmic eyes.

# My Own Zest

I have unlearned your skin,
that treacherous vine
encroaching my lattice
before the break of day —

its lilac draping
from my feeble gasp,
its scent of pitfall and campfire
the morning after.

And one day, I wanted to feel,
not your nod upon my flesh,
not your eyes anoint my chest,
but my own craving,
my own zest.

# Dormant Elegies

In your hands, the sky is a rag.
You lather me in clouds,
soak me in stars.

Trees exhale their privilege,
so I can waft
from satori to dusk,
to paradise.

Days are dormant elegies
that you revive.

You whisper tempests
upon my navel,
and bait them with one finger…
to pacify.

# All I Feel Is Art

You nest on my bosom
of quiet wilderness,
where one can hear a tear sigh
and songbirds die a proud death
upon my limbs,
love-struck and dignified.

You draw fresh bark
from a primed canvas;
my scruples fossilize.
My taste buds scrape
the astral zing,
so all I feel is art.

# The Dare

He dared me to break his heart,
for that would mean I touched it,
pinched it, stretched it,
and took it to the park—

tossed it, lost it, found it,
and held on to it tight.
Then dropped it, washed it, rubbed it
to make it clean and bright.

I thought him a bit masochistic;
now I know he is wise.

Part I: Portraits

# Mars

Sometimes a stranger
feels like home,
and I want us to land
on the planet we once occupied.

It is made of red rock and lilies
that shimmer against dry clay.
He is out hunting suns
to rein the day.
In the valley, I wash muddy stars
to adorn the night.

We lived on Mars.

# Little Nothings

I will kiss your face
as a statement of fact,
a pledge the wind might whisper
to a dormant pansy:

"I will thaw your frostbit sighs,
I'll reface your ombre petals.
I will lasso the tardy sun
to a tacit yearning,
until its warmth
dapples your stigma
and ignites your elan."

Part I: Portraits

# Fragility

Dread is... self-realizing,
like when I feared your touch
would keep me whole
as you held my fragility
with your fingertips.

I knew eventually
you would retrieve your hand
to scratch your nose,
and I would shatter.

I still let you reach.
I still let you leave.

# The Stunt

His love was not a promise
of Sunday brunches
or footsie-fights in a warm bed.

It was a cry of thunder,
a jerk of lightning
to warn me of the approaching rain.

His love was not a feeling
or an inkling
of things that merit time and space.

It was a stunt,
a mirage,
a could have been.

Part I: Portraits

# Sweet and Sour

I inhale you by inertia
through summer's enlarged pores —
a dormant mandate of latent love.

You live gaily in molecules
of dripping sweat,
and wind the sweet and sour
bends around my chest.

I taste you in salty drips
of midday sun
when brave rays singe,
and embers long.

# Drifting Whisper

Am I still within earshot
of your watchful heart?

Or am I a whisper
drifting through your aura
of musk and sandalwood?

Your eyes no longer find me
in lingering words
misspelled by clouds
in the desert sky,

but your gaze still burns
across the winter miles.

# Corrosive

Sunpatiens on my cheeks,
and your portrait pinned
on the hollow of another day...

I am empty of tears
that pool in the shallow
but brimming with salt.

It's corrosive where I am tender,
and cleansing in the space
you filled with whispers...

of trees commanding wind.

# Magnetic

My leaves trail your light,
proceeding in wonderment
after your grace,
craving that effulgence–
epiphanic in your eyes,
tumbling lithely
against your shadow,
and hiding in the chambers
of your mystique.

Part I: Portraits

# Doting Angel

If I could,
I would draw you in ink —
fill the night in your irises,
shade the space in your grin.

Rub *donaire*[2] on your hair,
chisel your chin,
sketch the bigger picture,
lithograph your mien.

Your face would be eternal.
Your mood, every being.
Your gaze, a doting angel
reaching through the mirror.

---

[2] *Donaire*: Spanish for grace and charm

# Yesterday's Sand

Find me when the tide goes out,
buried beneath your toes
with yesterday's sand.

My skin will be encrusted in quartz,
my grin diluted by blues and salt.

My memory will be deeply sunk
into sedimented grit
where nothing ever moves,
where nothing is ever moved.

# Blind Faith

And if your arm will bend
toward my angled elbow
to chaperone my loneliness,
I will confess…

that my eyes have failed me,
that I just can't see;
that my pores seek warmth
from a dying ember
before the silence,
and I can't read smoke signals
on cloudy nights,

but I do feel the tide.

# Rides

Trains and roller coasters
remind me of you,

how you rushed to get nowhere
with a godlike grin;

how you would flip me upside down
in an astral whim,

how you would never stop going—
out on a limb;

how I wished for endless rides
on your tireless vim.

# Trusty, Old Heat

As the years pass,
we become unruffled,
inured to hubris'
whirls and crumples.

Old personas drain in the wash
of one more laundry day.

We are fresh and warm,
no longer patching rifts
with conversation,
but smoothing wrinkles

with trusty, old heat.

# Where Todies Sing

Shadows hang to dry.
The day is aglow.
My breath has slowed.
Monsoons turned to drizzle
inside my eyes.

I notice little things,
how your stretched, suede hand
replaced "I love you,"
how you outsmart the wind
to fill my lungs.

How your colossal smile
bursts my understory,
where todies[3] sing.

---

[3] A tody (Todus subaltus) is a tiny, colorful bird endemic to
the Dominican Republic.

# Figure of Speech

I am not one to murdrum
the fringes of a palindrome[4]
or nullify a feeling
for fear of the burn.

I will melt the lemel
to isolate gold.
I will poleaxe a tenet
to find my core.

So, when you wow my pupils
with stunning words,
I guttle our story
and beg for more.

---

[4] How many palindromes can you find in this poem?

# Heart to Heart

You climb our bed,
after the silence.
Reticence knots your throat.

I brush your tenderness
with a silky voice,
and loosen your tightness
with fleshy bristles.

I braid your fears neatly
and tie them in a bow
of velvet whispers.

You bawl the night away
in my soundproof bowl.

# Frog Prince

I step away, but you lure me to your pond
with lilac and lace.

You draw me to your land
of linen and grace.

You lull me into a lollygag
with your embrace,

enthrall me with lilies,
lupines, and laurels.

Then, you go, leap into a lotus
and leave me in a haze.

# A Story

His hands, a story.
His eyes, a film.
Her curves, a journey.
Her lips, a sin.
His tongue, the scapegoat.
Redemption, skin.
Her nails, a pondering
of butter scraping bits.
His thoughts, a rapture.
Her words, his dream.
His will, her vowels
crumbling reverently…

# Je Ne Sais Quoi

When seconds pend
above the passive hours,
breath is a riddle
for something more,

an elusive thought
I almost caught
while hummingbirds
fought for nectar.

It is a dulcet driblet
dangling from a lucky guess.
It is a hanging secret...
a *je ne sais quoi de vous.*

# A Day in Hospice

I lost you in the conjecture
of a day in hospice,
forgotten to the immediacy
of grippier melodramas.

Convalescent,
it threw its two cents
to the pastel wall.

Its maternal ancestors
gathered around the bed,
tallying the elapsed seconds,
waiting for my exhale
to finally pass.

# Drenching Wave

Who can quell
a rising tide of impotence,
lathered in longing
at the feet of the past?

Nothing moves its mighty columns
or corrodes its concrete slabs.

Some would wish to bathe its toes
from dawn to gloaming.
Some will ride the drenching wave
and retreat with the low tide.

# Lucky

The night rings in my dreams,
churning and pressing from within.
I see you float over golden hills
and remember your charm:

how every key turned
for your supple hands
and angels guarded each door
so we could sneak behind,

how luck would follow you,
as though you were its guide.

# The True Color of Fall

She wore white the day he left,
instead of crimsons and mauves,
that early November.

Leaves had danced their ochre Vals
while she dragged her feet
through their crunchy walls.

Why not beam in acquiescence
like a docile dove,
or a flag compelled to undulations
when it can fight no more?

Red does not capture the humbling drop.
White is the true color of fall.

# The Trip

It is a gift—
how you unzip my malice
and presage indiscretions.

Your hands patrol
the roundabouts and the valleys.
My whims zigzag
between strawberries
and melting moons.

It is a trip—
how you beam me up
and pull me home.

# Courting the Empress

Realms nest within her bosom,
and a string of pearls tugs at her ear.
She dwells amply in her still lake,
adorned with lace,
softer the water for her fair grace.

If I called on her
she would not hear me.
I must leap into her chasm
if she is to see me.

She won't look up
for she is most high in darkest depths.
She won't look down,
for nothing is real beneath her love.

# Land on Me

Land on me, butterfly,
tenuous, fleeting, and seminal.

Flutter me labile
after your whims.

Emblazon me in hues
of sorcerous tint.

Flicker me alive.
Wither me extinct.

Molt me a dalliance
that hangs from your wings.

# Jaded Seraphim

I keep my distance
from that greenhorn angel
who wants me to feel alive —

to drop some burdens, to bite an apple,
to throw my gray hair into the sky.

I am drawn to a jaded Seraphim,
who broods in silence
behind dark screens.

He denies serendipity
but awaits the unforeseen.

# Paso Fino Horse

You fell for Venus one lucky night,
and I watched her beauty
soften your face.

I sensed her kindness
sober your eyes,
and her brightness
exhaust your dark.

I saw your gait,
like a *Paso fino*[5] horse,
on her straight line.

I saw a man
I would have loved,
had you been mine.

---

[5] *Paso fino* (fine step) horses are naturally-gated, light horses
imported to the Caribbean from Spain, prized for their
smooth riding.

Part I: Portraits

# Waterfalls

I went chasing waterfalls
down your spine…
of steep sighs and slithery obsidian.

I lost my bearings
at your narrow crest
and a choir of voices
muffled my fall.

I prayed for mercy
upon your sacrum
of wish and bone…

but gods could not make my words
over roaring water.

I drowned at your base
of sand and stone.[6]

---

[6] Originally published in Fevers of the Mind

# Winter

I remember him like a slap of ice
on my tender cheeks,
his crude hands scraping my skin
for his favorite shade of truth,
my exposed nerves
alive with anguish
for his probing whims,
and his reproach
I did not dress properly
for the bitter winter of him.

Part I: Portraits

# With or Without You

When I am with you,
I dance a smooth ballad.
My pace slows
to prolong the seconds.

The lyrics introflex,
but the melody spills outwards.
I arch, and twirl
tied to your fingers.

You push and pull,
but the tempo is mine.
You clear the stage
and retroflex time.

Without you,
I swing to merengue,
and salsa, and mambo
to my inner rhyme.

# Blank Chariot

I watch and hurt,
but yours is not my story to tell—
where you go in that blank chariot,
seizing seconds before they melt.

Someday, when youth becomes
a threshold of forlorn hours,
and the river gorge cascades,
you will know
I was present for your absence,
and that I hid it well.[7]

---

[7] Originally published in Fevers of the Mind under
"Absence"

Part I: Portraits

# Fireworks

A light flickered
for lurching ghosts in the dark.
They were busy sniffing birds,
keen on halcyon symphonies
and pleasing sights.

I, too, wandered the unlit realm
from night to night,
slurring nirvanas after each snake bite,
expecting fireworks,
and missing the sparks.

# Bonfire

Flames are candid.
Their truth is tangible. Their aura, warm.
It is why we build bonfires
on cool summer nights.
All of you gather around the pit.
The scolded child whimpers on your lap.
His face is taut with dry tears.
His lips tremble a nervous laugh.
Your younger self eyes you in reproach
for dreams you foundered on paper rafts,
and that summer garden
you would always promise but never plant.

Your future elders are also there.
Their eyes are blurred from the rubber
of many false starts.
Yet they smile a glinting nimbus
against dark skies.
They are here, willing and raw
from scrapes of possibility.
One by one they hold you.
Their embrace is soft around your fears.
Their words are balmy against your temples.
They lift your withered child
high above the sparks,
higher yet above regret.[8]

---

[8] Originally published in MasticadoresUSA

# Sweet Dreams

When you dream of me, you know
that joints light up
before muscles ache
and you will lick your fingertips
for the rare taste
of us.

When I see you in dreams, I know
a chiliad ways to blur the doors
so we can stay
home.

# Connected

I have my ways to find you
when fuzziness clouds my lense.

There is a soft snagged thread
hanging from my dress
to catch your quirky edges
and brush your jagged flesh.

There is a rare high pitch
in the night's lower frequency —
a vagary that jolts me
and shows you, by coincidence.

# Worn Down

You play peek-a-boo
on foggy mornings
when the world is an ache
outside my window

and I want to feel your hands
sand the jagged edges
off my withered skin

while robins tag along
with refined, love songs.

And I am too old for games,
but rivers flow in declension
toward their end.

With the same rush,
I step out of the frame.

# Fifteen

For precious minutes, we knead dry earth…
Grain by grain of affable clay.
Her face beams adobe and powder
on this rose gold day.

She is fifteen today. Lower heels boost her steps.
Gone are decades of love lost on unyielding mud
fossilizing her caring hands,
while ore built skylines on her fertile palms.

Gone is the silk that preened her dread.
She is dressed in steel before the blue.
She will lift waterfalls from their deep slump.

Today she climbs on mangy trees.
She rains on boulders and leaps upstream.
She dodged a supple death when it swung
from palm to pine to oak.

She watched as it hoarded wins
of gems shinier than words
and fruits juicier than youth.

She is fifteen today, not sixty-two —
not a grandmother, twice a widow,
not an olden labor of awe,
who lost her youth to privity and yet dreams.

# Excuses, Excuses

I would kiss you at daybreak,
but there is the sunshine,
swaddling my lips
with wisps of rouge.

I would meet you at sunset,
but there is the moon,
wagging her knowing finger
at the sky.

I would run away with you
but the dazed horizon
misplaced its line.

I would make a home with you
but burning forests
have lost their pine.

# Elements

Alliterations of you
pervade my fascia.

My chest is taut
but my hips loosen with assonance.

They sing cantabile in a rhythmic portal,
complete and partial.

I am gone, gone to this body
like an immortal.

And you are awake, present,
and consonant to your own aura.

# Pastries and Brew

I wished to befriend the morning
and rejoice
when it clapped on my window
with her demure spark.

Her toasty hands
would leaven my objection
to the wintry day.

I would brew with apprehension
at a life without you
while she bakes me scones
of promise.

# This Quill

This quill is leaden with replies
to questions you never asked,
trite scripts you would not trust,
fatigued emblems not worth redeeming.

So I took the plunge
and begged my mulish plume
to imbue its racy curves
with indelible meaning.

And I penned every love poem
from crepuscule to dawn.
I pled, urged, and succumbed
to seasons of dry ink.

There is nothing else to note,
no more wise men to quote,
no more itch inside my throat.
I left it all in this moat

of unvoiced feeling.

Part I: Portraits

# Inner Feminine

I know your feminine

in the way you await a move
before that first dance,
how easily my fingers weave
on your exposed hands,

how your thoughtful amble
often follows my gait,
how your quarter moon
anticipates my gaze,

how your heart will open
and close in a haze.

# Proud Birds

Beneath your sighs,
ribbons of blue
gather darkened skeins
about your neck.
Your throat, of braided candor,
is choked by an apple
higher than the proudest peak,
startling like doves
who clap their silent wants,
too shy for conversation.

# It Was Worth It

He wheedles moons for a lark,
digs his fingernails into the earth,
prodding for a temperature, or a rise.

He swims laps in her viscous magma
and floats like driftwood within her core.

She is awed by his gumption
and pretends not to know
that he will eclipse her sun.

# Mournful Dream

He stole a day from my reservoir.
It wasn't a nightmare,
more like a mournful dream.
My entire garden was pinned to a book
I wanted him to have.
Years passed before I watered it,
and it wilted,
not from hunger or lack of sun
but from his touch that left me
dry and forlorn.

# The Sea of My Flaws

Her face was on the wall,
drifting like a frigate
after a lost war
(in the sea of my flaws).

I let her go
to cast-net her paradox
upon restful shoals.

I am too listless to be drawn
by stoic ghosts
fishing for miracles
in long-tails of yore,
as I drown in comfort.[9]

---

[9] Originally published in FromOneLine Anthology, Vol. II

# Shadow Bride

In the darkness of daylight
fear dons all-white to meet the day.
Her long gown,
made of soft lace and doubt,
draws dirt.

She smiles a wary sunray
in the filtered shade
of all that is safe.
And her spouse,
pleased and proud,
dotes on her.

# Identity

I.

I am warm sand on the shore,
crystal bay water swaying ping pong.
My core is clay and coconut bowls
hidden by mangroves
of white-tailed folklore.
The goddess naps on my hammock
domed by dry palm,
with space for a floor.
I am a palmchat in a cottage
inhaling coffee and sweating rum.

II.

I am the hands beating my flesh
for achy music,
a pang of tenderness in their palm.
I am the song he wrote for me
one summer night.
The bells that startle my dominion,
the hope backstroking in the dam...
I am tomorrow's rueful echo,
rhapsodic history on a scratchpad.

Antonia Wang                    74

# Pockets of Night

Sometimes I trip
on my own shadow,
digging my heels
between pockets of night.

The sullen street lulls
beyond my window.

I take note of the moon,
ready for her gala,
dimmers on her gown
and blue on her face
from the monthly wait.

I no longer fault my fear
for its haste.

Part I: Portraits

# Manqué Cathedrals

Words slash like shards.

I shall evade grief threads
blasting caverns of rain
inside my brain.

I know the place enough
not to let knees and claws
clutch at the pain,

lest boulders weigh
manqué cathedrals
upon my back,

without dynamite
to clear the way.

# Blurring Footprints

Where the vines tangle
on the golden hills,
your smile unravels
from valley to sea.

And there are hawks
where your finger points
to bees and howling innocence.

So, I watch each butterfly
that flutters on your hair
and blur your footprints
while you prance and sing.[10]

---

[10] Originally published in FromOneLine Anthology, Vol. II

# Young Lady

Her vanity buds, bashful and cautious,
in early spring.

Then it bursts into pink blossoms
and lipgloss.

She pinches her cheeks for rouge
and folds her innocence on pleated skirts.

Tomorrow, she will draw idylls
on foothills of magic.

Hurry! Love!
before the goddess wakes.

# Did I Make You Up?

The horizon hankers
for the evening twilight,
when days cross the limen
that awakens ghosts.
I am afraid you will drown
in a wave of absence
far from these shores.

Love will clothe
unwholesome secrets
in silk and glamour.
I am afraid I will lose
the gist of your essence
in a metaphor.

# Eternity Ring

You handed me eternity
trapped in a ring
so I could thread infinity
with your growing soul;

but mortality is no blemish
for the ancient sun.

I will die on my love
bereft of avarice,
content with one more day
in your timid glow.

# Moon-struck Cafe

The day conceals her,
clad in lace.
She fades into a mirage.

She moves the oceans
inside your veins
while she pines for her night.

She flirts with poets in a noir cafe,
and paints crooked smiles
in their eyes.

She exudes tenderness
and beams with grace,
but no one sees her darker side.

# Moon Child

I cannot tell
if Jupiter expands my woes
or Venus brings me love,
if Mars trines my loneliness
or Saturn squares my bones.

I am a daughter of the moon,
relaxed in its shadow.
I spin blindfolded within its craters,
and when it pulls the tide,
I brace for impact
between your arms.

# Indescribable

I would dab your eyelids
with micellar water and rosehip lips.
I would curate the pixels
that tickle your pupils
at the water's edge.

I would snake the leaves
of a house plant
to sublimate your air.
I would forge the glimmer
of a dazzling star
to luster your hair.

In that intimate moment,
our chests would swell
an Everest summit
streaked in pastels.

An ineffable radiance
would drape the penumbra
in which we fell.

# Chimeras Don't Come Cheap

I offered pennies for your thoughts.
You never said a word.
I would offer you a dollar
but want to save some more.
Chimeras live and die
in covert limbos,
emblematic like carved stone.
They write our 3D stories
in cryptic lingos.
When they breathe fire,
all paper burns.

# At the End of the Day...

Looking away is no victory
when your neck writhes,
if you bathe in pride
while sitting on thorns.

Why strive
to keep a safe distance
if your veins ferry
her scent in your blood?

If your eyes are guided
by her golden lumen
and she ignites your nights
when blinds are drawn…

# Consolation Prize

He hands me a rose,
as if my fingers had not withered
when he took the sun,
and my palms had not bled bruised cardinals
who could not cheer a song,
as if red could promise
he was coming home.

He writes me a song,
as if notes could run the miles
from his pen to my home,
and words could cross the bridge
before it cracked and burned,
as if I knew the melody
after so long.

# Ever Here

You hide between a whimper and a tree,
but forget the thunder
scurrying beneath your feet.

The moment stalls
but for a blink of lighting
startling your pensive eyes.

Fire hides you in a ring.
The moon conceals you,
as if I don't know where you are.

You are here, always here,
treading a tightrope
in the midnight silence
within this lifeless cave.

Part I: Portraits

# Sawdust

When the day settles
on my eyelids,
heavy and restless,
I want your palms
to sand the jagged edges
of my withering skin.

Because the earth aches with stardust
from carrying us all,
and I am buried in sawdust
from too many thoughts.

# Implicit Rhyme

Maybe it is not your hands.
Maybe she breathes
to inspire crushed stars.
Perhaps her pen has an innate meter,
her voice an implicit rhyme.

She will not try
to interpret silence or decipher hearts.
Her blooms may wither
but she can still climb,
and bud on a dime.

Part I: Portraits

# Redundant

If I knew what to say,
I would say it once
and leave redundancy
in the hands of time.

I would watch you scratch the moon
for a slit of tenuous light,
and pray that fallen angels
can show me a path to God.

I would kidnap allegories,
and speak the truth at last:
I am only yours,
prolix and flawed.

# Snooze

There is no sun today.
The air is a blanket of honey mist,
and summer is tattooed
on my golden skin.

Trees are vaping,
blowing blue smoke.
Your voice anoints me
through the morning fog.

Dream catchers scream
but the astral fairies gleam
and my sleepy pillow moans
for one more hour.

# Back Where We Belong

I leaped,
for a fish out of water
longs to feel the breeze.

I gasped at your levity,
at the ease with which a feather
discerns the wind.

You would glide,
with the immense wingspan
of those who fly alone.

I returned to the sea,
where the air in my gills
is deeply personal.

# It's a Long Story

While we were apart, I quit playing chess.
I surveyed the rubble and cut off my chains.
I summoned my angels, cleaned up the mess.
I took a salt bath to recall my breath.
I dabbled in freedom, took a train West.

I met a sweet wizard who makes video games.
Then fell in love with Lucky and his dreamy
mane.
We detonated gondolas and rode bikes in the rain.
I ran into a brewmaster. He called me Red.
He liked to catch marlins in the Sea of Cortez.
He was fun and witty. We could have wed.

But I found a piece of driftwood at Stinson Beach.
His cool sand and water tickled my feet.
He built me a house from elephant ears
and filled my garden with baby tears.
I looked at the sky to thank the quarter moon
but time had lit her craters
and she, too, was full.

Part I: Portraits

# Part II: Landscapes

All I see is beauty. I am overcome with admiration
for nature's jailbirds: the fleeting derelicts who
stretch out untrodden paths for the heck of seeing
mother fret, and whom existence always rewards
with a destination.

# Garden Erotica

I.

He traced me where orchids blush
between carnation and mist.

The morning breeze was eros
brushing between my lips.

His thumb tinged my symmetry
with every shade of pink,

and I swooned on my sepals
before his simper and heat.

II.

I dream of lavender
in your blooming fields —

a whorl of wonder
in your pinnate lines,

a dueling couplet
giving me the feels,

and your flush corolla
laving my sepals.

Antonia Wang

# It Was Art

I don't regret the landscape
we painted blindly
on a young canvas.

Your careless strokes
degrading my fondness,
your bold hues
blurring my pastels.

I don't rue the lines
we drew with hubris
on that perpendicular,
unable to compromise.

It was messy.
It was genuine.
It was art.

# Capricorn

Where does one go without a torch
on a moonless night?

I built my summer home
across your Capricorn,
transversal strings of time.

You almost lost me
looking for your nodes
between the tower and the littoral.

I almost found you
wearing gold motifs
past the wistful meridional.

Antonia Wang

# Feels like Fall

The garden is dry ochre and pine,
piling words against still life.
It crackles gravity under my bare feet,
tickling my arches where love once hung
content to shift the ground
and ride the pranic winds
to the weary heart—
only to flee, crestfallen,
with the next exhale.

# Seasons

She will bloom dainty and bright,
constellations in the dark,
until autumn's final gasp.

Then she will sleep
a caramel-apple death at winter's feet.

She will dream a balmy earth
steeped in candor
and wake to his rain and thunder,
delirious spring.

Antonia Wang

# Bouquet

Petticoats in summer for this sudden chill.
Soft down over my head, for it is night still.

White lilies ladder to gather your light.
Carnations are a sort of genesis.

The sky is a lachrymose prism of blues.
Parched desert primroses suckle your hues.

Gardenias pale around your perpetual ring.
Moon-sung, gay robins disperse all your dreams.

They bait the rain and divert the wind,
so morning glories grow of their own free will.

And the encumbered zinnias wedged on the hill
delight your twilight when tedium rests.

Velvet and lavender fill golden chests
of your fragrant caress.[11]

[11] Originally published in Masticadores USA

# Señorita

Sometimes the river hums
one-way journeys for songs.
Mine was a brief susurrus
muffled by rain and rapids,
a barrage of garbled notes
finding their tune and tone,
a sigh of the proverbial
when destiny comes to bank
and it reaches its cupped palm,
calling nonchalantly: "*Señorita*."

Antonia Wang

# Clouds Are Pining

The eager sun will hum
his fiery song around the moon,
but his voice is brass —
burning silhouettes on thirsty grass.

Rain will storm the longing fields
and refill depleted gardens,
despite this act.

Nobody sings like rain
when clouds are pining.
Nobody drums like thunder
on wrathful skies.

# Collage

Nothing ever leaves my velcro chest.
Landscapes and portraits
cling to my tenderness.

I am a collage of nostalgia
and chirpy bird songs,
a scrapbook of postcards
and minor soul burns.

I am a baker of dreams,
and a butcher of words,
a black hole of memories
whirling for more.

Antonia Wang

# Stray Feathers

Poems are stray feathers
from ashen birds
who bepurple clouds
because they have wings.

Their dance is a litany
of futile flaps,
unworthy of sound
but for the moonlit sonnets.

They can cruise
a lonesome mile
above your gelid eyes
but you'll still feel their warmth.

# Fall Color

Change crawls from the fringes
into the crown —
with a balayage of questions.
They mature unspoken,
colored by resolve.
The unshakable will turn red
before surrendering,
enameled with longing
to the inexorable sunset.

Antonia Wang

# Heart Grows Fonder

Absence is endless wisdom
scurrying rock to rock
above the skin,
lurking in barkless trees
draped in vulnerability,
quiescent in toasty cavities
where death dares not a toe,
where love melts in incubation
and reforms to a silent murmur —
nursing the roots.

# Idyllic

Where are you, butterfly?
A thousand stories
invade my morning.

I settle on our toes,
dug deeply in the warm sand,
the suave Caribbean heat
telling us there is no rush.

My eyes blinded by dusk,
your pores craving sweet touch.
One hand on my waist,
your lips on nectar.

Antonia Wang

# Unseen

Oh, the profanity
of a day without touch!
Eden is withering
without twilight's glow —

for eyes can strip a rose
but cannot keep it warm,
and apples only grow
under the sheet of night.

Oh, the inanity
of beauty without judge!

# Widdershins

Sometimes worlds run amok
to the draft of quiet inhales.

Within them, we truly talk,
and ponder, and listen, and hear.

Astute birds guard these aery worlds,
slitting words thicker than air.

Time is an owl flying widdershins,
so when we say goodbye, our story begins.

Antonia Wang

# A Thousand Pines

We grew from saplings
of a thousand pines
planted with gusto
on the mountainside.

Our footprints on the hill,
dust and silt...
Infinite skydives can't liken the thrill
of dirt on my roots,

and your hands on my bark,
and your sap in my limbs
flowing so dearly,
so gently, still.

# Spirit Guide

On the horizon, peace is a line,
a forbearance of rage
before the high.

I am at the shore, the unruly curl
surging with elation,
ebbing to the shore.

I am free but for the moon.
She tugs my ponytail at low tide,
and drags me to my depths
like a good guide.

Antonia Wang

# Beauty Marks

Perhaps tomorrow
I will undress the moon,
highlight her craters
as beauty marks.

I will let you touch the jewels
in her cryptic box.
We will pause to hear her whimpers
when stars are low.

I will tell you wonders
when you can't hear me
over her doubts,
and wolves are a howl short of faith.

# Holding Silence

Silence is already a sly mockingbird
with wings agape,

gliding the baffled sky
for the perfect sonnet.

When it finds it, it nests on a line —
golden and never uttered.

It makes space for crescent dreams
from flimsy clutter.

It does not need you to set it free.
It wants you to hold it.

Antonia Wang

# Boulevard of Matte

The door was left open
to a boulevard of matte.

The city glints and dazzles
with blueberries in one hand,
arm in arm with the ocean
while ennui lurks behind.

Nights fan their restless charm.
Years saunter and pass,
inhaling air in sepia
with no heart for farewells.[12]

---

[12] Originally published in FromOneLine Anthology, Vol. II

# Salt Bath

I thought I would survive without you
swaddled in dunes, sugar, and sun,
befriending sirens at the midnight hour
to leave them by dawn.

I would scrub you away,
ground quartz on my pores,
and Yemoja,[13] heartbroken,
would thrust you offshore.

I thought I would love you
no more.

---

[13] Yemoja: Goddess of the Sea in the Afro-Caribbean
tradition

Antonia Wang

# Divine Dalliance

I must dance with the sea.
It will stir my cacao and coconut milk.

It will pull me in dull
and push me agleam.

Oh, divine dalliance,
everlasting tug!

Bury me in your sugar,
dab my lips with salt.

Clothe me with your turquoise,
and nothing more.

# Remembrance

The lighthouse is lifetimes away
but I can touch it with my goosebumps.
Windows open to the breeze
between your smirk and my blush.
A base of pale seashells
is tethered to the cranky sea.
Unwelcome seagulls at the market
nibble from dirt to sky
crumbling euphoria and delight.

Remembrance of scenes that played
only in the wistful heart.
A passage full of timelines
converging in one mind
carried by forceful waves,
tenacious to the last sigh.

Antonia Wang

# Autum Grass

He wrote me flames and blush
on an autumn note,
and I fell in his fountain
of purple and oat.

His ink, my yellow,
rustling those chill
November mornings.

He traced my silhouette
against the Beaver Moon
and my maiden tassels plumed.

# Tropical

I.

Waves are drinking the frothy moon
in moderation.
It is a tame, palm day
without snowflakes scraping
broody windows.
Calm now rains
between the crow and the horizon
but God retired to friendlier shores
storms ago.
I will miss her birthday
and her tropical candle breath
diluting wind.

II.

This will be the year I see you
wearing pineapple and palm,
donning sandals for a sun-kissed stroll
amid mangroves and sand.
and languid coconuts
lulled by a sea breeze,
draped in midday calm.
Sugar clouds become our hammock,
and whales christen us, as a reward.

Antonia Wang

# Unearned Privilege

I thrive on unearned privilege,
attuned to the earth's pulchritude
by way of keen eyes.
Her dulcet voice
acquaints my ears
with time's percussive pulsing
and the nightingale's song.
You almost touch me,
and a flicker of heat
crosses my window,
setting me ablaze.

# Summer of the Heart

The best shocks are open secrets.
Their scent is known —
asleep verbena and twilight notes.
It is still summer here.
My nose is stuffed.
There is no crisp morning air
but a mulish sun
peeling my heart after every rain.
Flash flooding shadows
cover my chest,
afraid I will bare it all.

Antonia Wang

# Liquid

I vaporized
in the summer of mistakes.
As I poured glib lines,
my goblet evanesced.

But I am liquid again,
miming mudras along with change,
lending trickles of sweat
to the thirsty breeze,

irrigating mornings
with gentle dew,
and nursing nascent creeks
on my way home.

# Your Wings in My Faith

This clichéd world,
where waves keep crashing,
clocks keep tapping
and the moon still beams
sapphic odes on your face...

The sun feeds your mornings
buttercup and cognac
while my lungs exert
to afford free air
and hummingbirds keep buzzing
your wings in my faith.

Antonia Wang

# Our Pulsing Flesh

We did this too, unnerve the sky,
beg for blinks of nourishment
and soothing cries.

We exhumed the roots
of a dying tide,
urging fading waves
to push us home,

wet with stigma
from cyclones of lust,
indignant at our pulsing flesh —

condemned to love, first and foremost.

# Sturgeon Moon

Twice in a Blue Moon,
when rods were questions,
sturgeons hummed
between catch and release.

Their song spread
with a mother of pearl spoon
over my tongue.

I tasted light from the Black Sea.
I touched its mollusks.
I watched the curves of the hourglass
bend to the dancing sand.

I felt your breath over my calm,
and your hands on my primal.

Antonia Wang

# Trust

For every drop that hurtles
down coaster hills,
there is a skydive ride
with air as swift as the heart.

And I trust your void
to catch me when my gut sinks.
I believe your palms
can halt my daily qualms.

And when hurt furrows
snips of doubt upon my dreams,
you will be my wings.

# From Within

You search for waterfalls
at the bottom of the cup
and watch her bathing nude
at twelve o'clock.

A bird on a ladder
braids the day's dainty filaments.

And joy is immanent
as it thunderclaps your mornings
with wide-winged angels
and mountain dew,
for she is with you.

Antonia Wang

# Bonfires and Sandbars

In a sea of faces,
you beam your eyes
until the racket drowns
beneath their light.

I tiptoe your reefs
to the coastline,
while you warn me of tricky shoals
during high tide.

I pirouette the length
of your sandbar,
and you build me a bonfire
to shame the stars.

# Know Your Dark

Do not heed the fickle morning
when it lures you,
promising a splendid day.
Her exuberance will cower
with the faintest rain.

Believe the night as it befalls,
obscure and frank.
It leans on the polished chatter
of waking owls and only asks
that you know your dark…

and walk those empty caverns
without a lantern or marker in sight.
When you find your refulgence
amid the gloom,
be thankful for the insight.

Antonia Wang

# River of Goods

When your fingertips brush
this silent feeling,
serpentine stories clash.

Do not prod me gently
through inert stained glass.

You dip your bullish toes
in my river of goods,
and let the waters part.

For you command my rage,
my rapids and depth
with your quiet art.

# Saccharine Death

It is a pleasure, and a curse—
the way your fingers course,
the rivers and roads
of my treasure hunt.
It is a honeysuckle pinch,
a saccharine death,
a wild blueberry twinge,
spicy-vanilla-pink
on my dianthus bed.

Antonia Wang

# Undercurrent

On the days the wind won't croon,
foreign echoes stalk my grotto.
An offbeat canary learns its tunes
from the crab moon.

I suckle from the mild earth
her liquid manna.
And you simmer underground
your ardent lava,

searching for open wounds
to feed me a world in an outburst.

# Firmament

In my mind, you are made of clouds
thumping lightly to thunder.
Your face is a firmament,
blue from music,
blushed with wonder.

Your hands are shields
that keep me safe,
from your eyes' torrential rain,
and in suspension, I remain
in your realm out yonder.

Antonia Wang

# Fun and Games

Stains on the horizon,
a sacramental metaphor,
and dark reflections
where nothing stands...

We still build treehouses out of loneliness
where the moment has passed.

Our footprints are scarlet stamps
seen from beyond by the oversoul,
who smiles wryly
as we play in the past.

# Everything We Planted

Why should we write
sullen elegies
to seeds buried in haste,
under the moon's fertile eyes
and the sky's misty mane?

Why look down,
crestfallen,
when dry soil loves free rain
and for every inhumed intention
saplings sprout for our gain?

Antonia Wang

# Ancient Wisdom

I hugged a tree last night.
I wrapped my mind around its bark.
I held my cheek against its brokenness,
and swung my leg over its wrath.

It held me back.

It said my pencil is inelegant
as I sketch the path.
That there is no need to paint over
what time has scratched,
that palettes hang on my periphery
rich with hues I have yet to find.

# Chronic Pine

We look but rarely see
beyond the stoic, chronic pine.
Snow-capped dreams on the horizon
form a vague, untrodden line.

Clouds will linger over peaks,
as if pointing to the path.
We count notes but rarely play.
Life's true melody outscores math.

Antonia Wang

# A Metric Moon

A cackle and a call,
a clapback of color
to the sparrow's song...

Perfect days unravel,
sultry as the sun
fondling my eyelids.

You want to know
why birds must nest
when they are obliged to the wind,

why purple lets yellow
ruffle its edge,
why I love you a metric moon.

# This Quiet Wish

Living between rainbows,
this quiet wish
dresses Rudbeckias in mahogany
for the summer ball.

She feeds goldfinches
ablaze with wonder
dark chocolate cones,
and bathes hot cardinals
in holy water
from the waterfalls.

Antonia Wang

# Share the Light

Pink magnolias and aloe vera stars
portend great beginnings.
Mornings blush pastel and soft,
before a racy sky.
The sun muffles my every thought,
so I discern with closed eyes.

On those days,
I wear yellows and whites—
nothing black that could absorb the light.
It must pass through me
and keep others warm.

# A Course in Magic

Watch valiant pansies
stare down Winter
with their sunlit faces.
Flex pain out of your hips.
Split a cheerful Sunday.
Squat by the river.
Gather flat pebbles.
Paint them into frogs.
Kiss one in its tiny mouth.
Open your arms and love!

Antonia Wang

# What Gives You Life?

Show me the clarity of your virgin will
and the carat of your buried dreams
when exposed to light.
I saw them sparkle in a side-glance
when you summoned their chi.

Let's go mine these rocks, impalpable,
and scratch their belief,
that they may morph into glossy gems
for us to tickle their thrill.

# Gratitude

Before the day ends
with a twitch of burnt orange,
I cradle my words
and kiss them to sleep.

I pair them by sound
on snug, handy clouds,
and pencil my love
to the sky in between.

I iron my blessings
with prayer-hand steam
and pin all my debts
where they can be seen.

Antonia Wang

# Open Deltas

I have written enough verses
to well stray clouds,
and build our boat
bit by bit.

but drifting words are only happy
when they reach the sea,
and emeralds ponder upon your irises,
and I can't tell what they can see.

Love sails grandly in open deltas
unknown to me.

# Back to Basics

I once wanted the truth.
All I got was frothy silence
crashing against my feet,
the white noise of acquiescence
blurring those vapid lines
drawn pointlessly, with hubris
on the oblivious sand.
Now, all I want is a warm ocean,
and your tender hands.

Antonia Wang

# Glide

As if I needed a reason
to skirt the skies when paths are long,
you sew me brand new wings
from silken moons, and golden orbs.

And I glide like a thought
on slippy yesterdays,
and sketch new rainbows
in monochrome.

I trace infinity above your cottage
with starlings in murmuration,
an octave above messenger doves
yet, miles below blue angels chasing love.

# How Love Blooms

Had I remembered
how urge refracts in your eyes
on arid days,
I would have spurned the rain.
But love blooms in its own garden
as it casts a rainbow —
shedding color on dreary skies,
growing iris where the soil is dry,
sprinkling red on immaculate stars.

Antonia Wang

# The Wind

On summer mornings,
he greets me cooly,
chancing fingers up my spine.

He teases my auricles
and queues a mixed tape
of leaf rustles and chimes.

He pierces my breath,
meanders my legs,
and jockeys my arcs
with every ride.

He smells like Romeo
and tastes like pineapple
on balmy nights.

# Honeyed Pores

Daylight seeps into purblind nights,
dripping slowly into my honeyed pores.

I imbibe the southern air
with a boba straw,
and learn about harmony
from a live oak
as it leaches olden wisdom
into lazy moss.

*This* is when I knit my poetry,
and stretch my toes.

Antonia Wang

# Keep it a Secret...

that when the hilltop wanes
into eventide lows,
nightingales storm your lair
brooding for your waiting dame.

That unsaid words rumble
inside your bolted mind.
That your will jerks and crumbles
as you hunger for her eyes.

# If Canyons Could Talk...

As I blinked,
I thought I saw you
tie a worn message
to a carrier dove.

"Figs have borne fruit.
I never stopped loving you.
Red rocks still loom
over tearless land.

The canyons are silent,
my faith still plummets,
and years grow layers
on my barren heart."

Antonia Wang

# Lokah Samastah...

There is an oasis, a pristine shelter,
beyond the limen of a chaste thought–
a petal of virtue, strong as a fortress,
for a moment of grace.
In that rapture, I sense only love.
I see arms that lift you to bliss and repose.
I see your true splendor,
and pray that you feel whole.

*Lokah Samastah Sukhino Bhavantu*[14]

---

[14] The Sanskrit phrase *Lokah Samastah Sukhino Bhavantu*
means: May all beings everywhere be happy.

# How Can You Melt?

How can you melt in the rain
when your skin is obsidian,
if dew rides on your aura
and dips your meridians?

When clouds part above you
so everything is bright,
and elephant ears
capture your light…

If gardenias in blossom
steal fragrance from your belt,
how can you melt?

Antonia Wang

# Green Light

It rains in pixels
at winter's edge.
It is easy to mistake
eager daffodils for naïveté.

But nature has safeguards
against false starts:
a bit of coddling,
an afternoon nap,

a Jacob's ladder
enabling the foolish,
aiming just a bit more light
at those who dare to try.

# Beauty Can't Hide

Beauty hides in a spray of roses
to sign off for the day.

It would gladly rest,
were fragrance not a giveaway.

It hitches a ride on a yellow butterfly
to ponderosa pine.

It bathes in a lake for it has a date
with the blowing wind.

It sneaks in your breath
to aromatize your chest, and abide

in subtle realms
I can't describe.

Antonia Wang

# Chaperoning Dreams

Gold shines brighter
at the end of the rainbow,
amid idle clouds
chaperoning dreams.

It is there I often find you,
restoring the day's glint
with dish soap and water,
riding nuances between indigo and violet.

Your magenta braids are streaked
with gradual change.
Your demure smile is a benediction
of red for the blue.

# I Still Remember

You look at me
as if my river ran on your course,
and you knew my delta
and my source,
my depth and my rapids.

But water time warps
and tells me stories
of when my wings were dawn,
my eyes were fire,
and my heart, an echo
of your candid voice,
which danced in a spiral,
insisting: "I'm yours."

Antonia Wang

# How We Bloom

Nature flaunts, and I like to watch
all that flourishes
with a little bit of warmth.

Azaleas kiss the ground
while their coy leaves drown
in waves of pink and white.

Blackberries bud, like roses
but become pregnant with sun.
Birds build snug nests
to incubate their young.

We bloom from fondness,
and peak in love.

# Too Amused to Hate

I could fight the tide,
dig my paws in the sand
and roar at the waves;
but I am amazed by their zig and zag,
tickled by the smug horizon
who pulls them nonchalantly
and dismisses them to their fate:
to rise, to sizzle, and fade.

I am too amused to hate.

Antonia Wang

# Retirement Plans

After all of this fades
into the chalk of an aging canvas,
we will emerge,
fresh from the mangroves
of a quaint island.

We will crisp
in the tropical breeze,
lying silent.

You will lave me with mangoes,
dry me with palms.
We will kiss until sunset,
and blur in the sand.[15]

---

[15] Originally published in FromOneLine Anthology, Vol. I

# Why Hearts Won't Heal

Time incarnated
for the sake of dancing in the rain
in early spring.
It heard it could
from a wingless fabulist.

It plays all summer
with winged sapphires
and perches gemstones,
away from forest fires.

It turns ombre in the fall
and flakes in the dead of winter.

That's why hearts no longer heal.

Antonia Wang

# The Magnificent Mile

Grapes will sizzle in your blood
a magnificent mile,
while you cycle toward love
on a Friday night.

We are far from heaven,
but close to Napa
and the amiable coast.

The journey winds and meanders
when your hand is my home,
and I don't mind
that we are lost.

I shine in your irises.
You live in my stride.
I am your vineyard
and you are my guide.

# Water Sign

My quest, like that of water, is
to not lose myself in the things I meet,

to not inflate the soil
as it grows its seeds,

to not reflect the moving earth
while I stand still —

to not shrink and evanesce
into the air I breathe,

to not feed the ocean
as it forgets about me,

to not quell the lonely fire
brewing storms to set me free.

Antonia Wang

# Ever Pine

From where I stand,
clouds are but a backdrop
for Southern Pine,

a wishful acquiescence
of gray and white
over glad skies.

From where I stand,
driveways and gates lead
to that same pine,

the unremitting green
shielding the land
from our transient lives.

# Part III: Still Lifes

I come aglow within you like a trail of hanging lights in the penumbra. You won't sense my luminance until you feel my warmth.

# Empty

I am empty of afternoons
that dawn at my window,
suggestive but subtle
in everything they hide.

My skull melds in the frame,
my back is shored by pillows,
and the sun cuts sharply
in my languorous eyes.

This scintillating lie
chimes in my ears
with incongruous kisses
where inertia bides.

I am drained from vacuous nights
canoodling billows
while stars plunge unnoticed
from an untethered sky.

# Headroom

There is headroom in the attic.
A nursery of bare verses
is watched by spider webs.
There are two bubble-wrapped oases.
One is a beach. The other, a bed.
There is a stack of kisses I never gave you,
and soothing stories I told myself.
My child drinks the empty words
and goes to bed.

There is an orange tabby
kneading my yearnings,
four friendly mice holding my breath.
They eat the spine off ancient books
to give me strength.
There is a candle scenting hours,
and an old clock sketching sunsets.
Its leaden hands tuck me in
without protest.[16]

---

[16] Originally published in MasticadoresUSA

# Feast

I have no wants,
for cicadas fill lacunas
with their hymns and hums,
my irises bathe in amber
watching the seasons fall.
I fill my basket
with blue mist and mums.
Half-bitten apples
feed songbirds their sun,
and you always find my table
when you are starved for home.

# Dancing Deasil

My clock has no hands,
so I began dancing deasil
around my own light —
a jaunt through life's boardwalk
with glee and panache.

I raked the withered days
in my jaded yard.
I played kiss or dare
with the hourglass,
and gave a death stare
to the tawdry past.[17]

---

[17] An earlier version of this poem was published in
FromOneLine Anthology, Vol. I.

# Wrinkles Won't Tell

There is a lumen on my nightstand,
and a shame of roses
wilting my cheeks.

Years sag against silk sheets,
untold apologies
dry-crumble far beneath.

Did I hunger for your lush,
indulgent touch?
Did I count every full moon
without your hands?

Stars stopped spinning
at your command.

# Quiescent Elegies

In the silence, static moans
quiescent elegies unheard by most,
but you tune to the requiem
of all unsaid,
because of a heavy heart.

In that cacophony, I lie awake,
in a fragile bubble
of soap and breath,
unharmed by probing fingers,
and your voice.

# Only Now

There are no tomorrows
in fear's aftermath.
Time has shut its noble arches,
so you stand idly by.

There is no more past
afflicting your step,
tugging at your clothes
to burden your face.

There is only Now,
flamboyant and suave,
pointing to the moment,
tempting you to act.

# Free Will

Choice spans two latitudes and a shaking head.
That's the extent of my regret.

A clink of glass or your searing eyes
simmering between my ears,

bundles of my favorite things
that came so easily when I received,

crops that grew ripe and plump
only in my caring hands...

And my face turned toward warming light
even as yesterday froze on my back.

# Rendezvous in the 5D

Silence hisses the dark of days
inside my ears.
Leaves stopped rustling
their stillborn green
outside my window.

There is no word in sight.
My vantage point from this fishbowl
is as clear as night.

So you alight my dreams
where we can gleam
in the astral glide.

# Doodles

Let me draw you a sphere
limned with light,
a realm of magic effigies
and archetypes,

an encounter with essence
two vibes apart,
a day of garden fairies
who farm new stars.

# A Shell like a Vault

I have no sad tales for your sympathy.
Or I do but refuse to show.
Pain is sweet under my tongue
as it jams my throat.

My eyes would flood
if the glaciers melted
inside my blood.

I would write the truth
but my quill is dry
of ink and shock.

It breaks my heart
that nobody knows me
although I've said so much.

# Read and Forgotten

Someday, I will come up with more
than a dry heave of verses
embittering my throat.

You will cast a sideways glance
at the bursting supernovas
that are visible through your curtain.

They will implode in a blink
and settle as dust on your clueless palm,
to be blown with unspoken reasons
that rarely rhyme.

# Ode to Source

I nibble on your feast
of orange and spice.
I nap on your bosom
of carbon and light.
I run on your fields
of jasmine and pine.
I dream on your sphere
and wake in your mind.

I paint on your canvas
of thought, space, and time.
I borrow your templates
and hone archetypes.
I trace your horizon
over my warped lines.
I die in my silence
and live in your light.

# The Sun Sang for Me Once

It beamed me into its crown
of golden filigrees.

I emerged a ray,
got to feed a leaf.

I dazzled the sky
with graffiti.

You looked my way,
turned blind,

and could not help
but close your eyes.

I died in your irises,
became a spark.

And there I live,
fickle and bright.

# Summer Wreath

I.

Birds are chirping but I am spent
from luring them to the veranda.
They perch on the wreath
I weaved with dried hope,
and restless hydrangeas
stuck on a thought.

Tomorrow, they will nip on Dahlia
and banter with Zinnia,
shunning conundrums
before resting
on a budding wish.

II.

I made a moony wreath
from lavender sighs and docile daisies
wired on a grapevine.
It limped infinity and came to hang
on your mahogany door.

Finches sieged the petaled throne
with fragrant symphonies.
They sit and wonder
who can bear lockdown
in your entropic home.

# Refuge

A half-hidden path
bares her shoulders
to passersby.

Her chest heaves under my feet
to antagonistic memories
of belonging and heartache,
petrified.

And I bathe in vestiges
of distilled light,
sluiced with kindness
by the Earth's sage silence
on strident days.[18]

---

[18] Originally published in FromOneLine Anthology, Vol. II

# Open the Windows

Swirling leaves of sage
predicted a purge,
a stark surrender
of what does not serve —
a solemn expelling
of "was" and "could have been."

To heal is to cleanse.
Release with a wisp
to dust and smudge
all the hidden corners
and sticky webs
to make room for happiness.

# Memento Mori

At the last moment,
old ravens perch,
and egos fade
into bright, white light.

Stories burn from the heat
of a magnifying glass.

Vanity whimpers
inside a broken mirror,
and finality tramples pride.

An angel serves you
a last, soft meal
while lilies bloom
at your gravesite.

# Living for Tomorrow

We shall see if the years grin
when the moment winks to heaven,
avid and bold.

Maybe they'll nod pridefully
as magic engulfs the seconds.

Maybe they'll cast a furtive glance
at wistful yesterdays,
when euphoria filled their chest
with pure nirvana,
oh, sweet love!

# A Poet's Prayer

May my thoughts be lithe,
slight like a book of verses
held by a biblioklept
stealth against the light,
subtle as impermanence,
anxious for a soothing line
to expiate my sorrows
if only while pages last,
to invoke from spilled prose
a fleck of my beloved.

# Before poetry...

every quill was dry,
all the prose was wry,
every dusk was brazen.

Butterflies were moss,
Jupiter was lost,
and the moon was jaded.

Flowers were red or yellow,
not crimson or mellow,
and their hopes were fading.

Muses were lonely maidens.

# Flower Moon

Do you see me plucking petals
from the flower moon?
She does not seem to mind.

With every pull,
she gets more bloody,
gives off a bit more light.

What will she tell the sun
when he calls for her at night?
She may hush me with a wink
and ask for a sip of wine.

# The Creator's Signature

All I see is you.
You whisper mornings awake
and fill my tub with liquid wonder.
You inhale wisps of coffee,
for warmth fuels your chariot.
You lift me gingerly with a thought
and in your thoughts, I levitate.
I plant smiles in your garden,
and they spread in adoration.

Part III: Still Lifes

# Ancestral Relic

An idle spear irks my marrow,
naive to time's hasty stroll.
It's an ancestral relic, slight and narrow,
forged from mirrors, dipped in gold.

A silk cotton canoe sails in my blood,
with specters of a sunset tribe.
It carries dry cacao, boiled taro,
and crushed *Zemís*[19] in Mahogany pipes.

And my grandmother's eyes
sunken in kindness
checking my garden for mint,
sage and pine.

We hold astral meetings
at the apothecary.
She teaches me remedies,
and I teach her rhymes.

---

[19] A zemi or cemi was a deity or ancestral spirit, and a
sculptural object housing the spirit, among the Taíno
people of the Caribbean.

# On the Way Home

Time is not an exotic melody,
nor the gods' tacit signature
pulsed by a metronome.
It is not a chorus, a verse,
or even a song.
It is our inherent prosody.
It's the rhythm of our soul—
the whom and what
consumed our hours
on the way home.

# Eternal Spring

I hail from eternal spring
in the Caribbean Alps,
where Iberians rolled their dreams
in tobacco, and worked the land.

Their days were homegrown coffee,
poetry, and fervent psalms.
Their gait was *pasodoble*,[20]
and so was their dance.

Men were dry and proud.
Women, shrewd and fine.

---

[20] Pasodoble (translated as double-step) is a fast, duple-meter, march-like Spanish style of music and its corresponding two-step couple dance.

Antonia Wang                    194

# Inner Child

My bedroom fades to sable.
So goes my mind.
Your words carve out a window
of LCD light.
I see the childhood ogres
I never had to fight.
My hologram was wholesome.
My angels, dignified —
but there was certain freedom I lacked,
a slight reproach
that trimmed my urge to fly.

# The Well

All we have felt
comes from a well
that only seems dark
for it isn't near.

Dawn lights the seconds
as the muck dispels
but it may take lifetimes
to note the water is clear.

And love dwells in ample springs.
It wets the ground and stacks the bricks.
It knits the rope, tightens the knots,
and gives you a bucket,
so you may draw.

# Silent Treatment

I.

He fed me absence instead of tenderness.
Succulents absorbed the silence.
He tucked his love under his sleeves.
It petrified his bones.
He starved me of words, bliss, and sun
when he aimed to try me.
I stacked my blessings upon his shadow.
He can no longer find me.

II.

Someday, when we speak the same language,
he will come to me if the sky turns orange,
and we will shame the sun into hiding.
I will not name the hues
depicting his aura on a clear day.
We will sit silently, our hands to the rain,
and watch the canyon fall into a dazed forever.

# What Lies Beneath

We lead double lives.
One limps heavily
from market to market,
picking fresh fruit on Monday,
and mauve blush on Friday.
The other swims in a stream
from wish to wish,
plucks weeds from invisible meadows,
and dips its fingers on the sticky past
for a taste of honey.

# Fog Is a Gauge

We misjudge the fog.
It obscures the road on a summer day,
until we can't see.
So, we hear trees soughing
in the Headlands,
and the Bay urging us not to stop
to bewail our life,
while giving a furtive glance
to a rusty bridge.
So, we go on
and drive the golden hills
in blind faith.
Fog is a gauge.

# Maybe It Was Love

Built on a hunch,
our days were *asana*[21] and Sol Food.[22]
Our evenings, Iron and Wine
upon wood floors.
Our spines ached from the bend
of an old guitar,
so we never moved.

Or maybe it was love,
etched in our columns
from the base of thought
to our sacred,
keeping us still.

---

[21]Asana: a limb of Yoga that consists on practicing a series of postures.

[22] Sol Food: Puerto Rican restaurant in the San Francisco Bay Area, CA. Not to be confused with soul food.

Antonia Wang

# Longing and Loss

We sing platitudes to its prowess,
the way it frolics with our hearts
on a Tuesday…

but rain surrenders to the thirsty plains
by its own measure,
and longings link us to loss
through their ubiquity.

Love lives blithely,
and sleeps softly,
in scanty harbors
between the two.

# Good Things, Tiny Doses

A hint of luck in treble waters,
a bit of black on honey bees,
a pinch of sexy on your modest,
a dab of humility on your preen...

A blush of pink on the horizon,
a nip of fervor on your cheeks,
a blot of sin to blush your holy,
and a quaver of joy in your hips...

A splash of ocean on your rear,
a slap of butter on your skin,
a slab of strength to last a year
and a sliver of moon on your grin...

# Bucket List

In no particular order,
I would like:

to peel the corona
off the arduous sun
and expose its flair,

to reacquaint with life
over jazz and rum,
and her spouse, Chimera.

to dine in sweatpants
(tie-dye and rose)
on the French Riviera.

to float in your moonshine,
melt in your salt,
and spark golden eras.

# Guilt

The happy muse makes an entrance
when draperies draw
cavern-deep and flowing freely.
She is flickering-candle soft,
yet steadier and brightest
when oxygen runs low.

Should I spread her glow?

Threading lightly feels like privilege
to the ragged robe.
I am bereft a heavy head
from guillotines of pain,
and were I not dressed in Teflon,
I could not withstand the flames.

# Another Wise Owl

Wisdom exerts a price.

The owl's lids sag with night
as she peers through worn love pleas
and silent prayers stifling the air.

Mumbled longings become cacophonies.
A litany of grief and blessings
muffle the agony
of arbitrary trips around the sun.

So, she hoots in response.

# Just Cry

A sob is lost
among the peaks and cliffs
of your jagged landscape,
where echoes squall
and quickly stall.

Sighs will birth
an ecosystem of anguish
where tears lurk.

And if they were to flow,
a lotus may emerge
and soften the edge.

# Irony and Metaphor

What is lost to irony
cannot be found in metaphors.
If dahlias were carnivores,
I would waft my fears
around its petals,
so they would gnaw my flesh
and sup my blood
every time the wind delivered me.
I would dicker with their fractals,
looking for imperfections...
only to find magnificence.

# Tweeting Birds

It is hard to know what is real
in this virtual age,
I strain to hear your voice
over tweeting birds;

but truth will rain monsoons
on calm, summer days,
where silence reigns like lava
over wintry haze.

# The Middle Way

If you need lullabies,
rock your arms to comfort.
Run a hundred miles
on Earth's own feet.

If you lose your breath,
move your dazed torso
in revolved half-moons
to salute the wind.

And when you tip the scales,
bring yourself to justice.
Stand in the middle
and simply breathe.

# Labor Pains

Things form long before conception.
Ideas are merely labor pains.

I saw a child in my mind's eye
before I knew men.
I named her "mine"
and so she came.
Where she goes from here
is her domain.

I had books in my womb
before I held a pen.

# Nothing to Say

Words come easy, so I pen
but there is nothing I need to say.
I accept time's tacit cadence,
the way it settles nature's debts.

A leaf will fall, snowflakes melt,
and moments fractal to your name.
Silence begs for proof of fondness,
and tulips slowly resurrect.

# The Rosary

It is wise to spy on Earth
as it circles dusk,
and catch her in the act —
of stuffing looted caverns
with yesterday's beads.

What more to fill the space
than unanswered prayers,
unheard Hail Marys
churned to gold in El Dorado,
polished, and glinting
for those craving hope.

# Dirty Windows

Some grieve tornadoes
and roaring thunder,
wailing at startled crows.

Some sip pain early
and hot with breakfast,
saving tears for a late lunch.

Some sleep with fragrant roses
and wear gloves to pluck their thorns.

Some glare at their dirty windows
wishing for a clearer world.

# Undying

Uncountable, the roads
lost to blurry hours
and feet running merrily
toward bright dead-ends.

Unbearable, the memories
that violate scarce seconds,
sagacious and profound,
bursting through fresh skin.

Untamable, the thoughts
beating the morning rush,
with coffee and reproach
brewing first thing…

Untimely, the love
that feeds on hearty silence,
undying but unable
to bloom in early spring.

# Wets like Love

Someday,
someone will catch the sun
glazing the sky with aurora,
blushing tomorrows
over the horizon.

They will be showered in light—
the kind that wets like love,
and waits like hope,
and fills like faith—
pouring Orenda
over their name.

I hope it's you.

# Acknowledgments

To Ty Gardner, for lending his poetic eye and keen attention to detail to this collection. As an admirer of his poetry and wordplay, I am honored he agreed to edit *Palette*.

To Anthony O'Brien, who continues to design stunning covers for my books. I appreciate his talent and professionalism.

To my family, for providing a peaceful and inspiring environment where I can reflect and write.

To the writing community on Twitter, in particular, the #vss365 and #FromOneLine prompt organizers, who helped inspire early versions of many of these poems with their prompts.

To my readers…

Thank you!

# Illustration Credits

# About the Author

Antonia Wang (pen name: tuttysan) was born and raised in the Dominican Republic, where she began writing romantic prose at an early age. She is the author of Love Bites, In the Posh Cocoon, Hindsight 2020 and Retrospectiva 2020.

Her poetry has been published by various online magazines and featured in the following anthologies: VSS365 (2019), Midnight With Words: Late Night Conversations in Poetry (2021) and From One Line, Volumes I and II (2021).

Antonia writes in English and Spanish. She has a background in Marketing/Communications, is a seasoned yoga practitioner and a certified yoga instructor. She lives with her family in the United States.

Website: www.biteslove.com
Twitter: @tuttysan

www.ingramcontent.com/pod-product-compliance
Lightning Source LLC
LaVergne TN
LVHW091216080426
835509LV00009B/1022